My Path is

Yoga in daily life

By Samnyasin Sādhvī Hridayakamal Puri

Impressum:
„Yoga in daily life"

ISBN 3-937082-51-4
The pictures from his Holiness Mahamandaleshwara Paramahansa Swami Maheshwarananda Puri Ji (Swamiji), Dharma Samrat Paramahansa Madhavananda Puri Ji (Holy Guruji), Shri Mahaprabhuji Deep and Shri Devapuri Ji are from the Organisation of „Yoga in daily life" and Swamiji's books.

Some are from friends and me.

Contents **page**

In thankfulness and love to my Master His Holiness Jagadguru Vishwaguru Mahamandaleshwar Paramhansa Swami Maheshwarananda Puri Ji, I am publishing my thoughts.

Through His great and divine teachings, His love, His patience, His protection and understanding I was able to understand and to fulfil my life dream, to renounce.

Thank you very much to Professor von Mackensen und to all my friends, for the patience to correct my English and to force me to publish my thoughts and my starting experience on the spiritual path.

Sadhvi Hridayakamal Puri

His Holiness Jagadguru Vishwaguru Mahamandaleshwara Paramhansa Swami Maheshwarananda Puri Ji. I am standing next to Him

I am standing in front

I would like to swim
I am standing in front
In front of it

This day today is a very special one
This day today has something special to be
I know today there is a special message for me
On a day like today you are one with everything

The longing to swim to dive deep into it
The longing to swim to feel I am one with it
The longing to swim to give my whole being to it
This longing is immensely strong today

So strong that my knees are getting soft
So strong that I have the feeling I will faint
So strong that I just wait
For the next big wave to jump into it

It is coming and it has a white crown
It is stretching itself so high and then
It is bowing down

Still I am standing on the beach when the wave
Is kissing my feet and my longing
to be one with the ocean is so immensely strong

I stand on the beach in the sand and enjoy seeing
The next wave coming towards me
And decide this one should carry me

Before the next one is coming to me
A big warning is rising in my heart
A big warning don't go too far
A big warning from the ocean towards me
Please respect me and don't dive today

My heart is telling me
Please respect and adore the ocean
Please control your feeling and do respect this message
It is a special message for you

My knees are still soft
My longing to swim and to dive is so strong
But I decide not to go in today
I decide to meditate on it
Then I know that I am part of it

After a while I look at my feet
And I see the ocean has presented to me
A shell, a white shell with the shape of a horn
And it has many orange hearts on it

I can see that the ocean also respects and loves me
Otherwise maybe I will drown
On such a special day
But God is in it and also within me
God didn't allow it to be.

Too late

You see an animal
And you do not know it
You see it is moving
You think why do I have to run towards it?
You are stressed
You are not able to move mind and body
But you would like to act
You would like to make yourself safe
And in this stress you think,
I will simply kill it!
The animal knows exactly
What will become of it.
It screams to you LOVE, LOVE, LOVE!
But you cannot understand its language
You don't know what it means
You don't know what it is telling you
And you were about to kill it
Now it cannot move any more
It is quiet and still
Now you are really able to see it
You start to turn it, and roll, and wind it
And you can find only beauty
You cannot find any poison
Now you feel very sorry
And you ask that it shall forgive you
But it is already dead
And it is

Too late

Asanas

Every cell, every drop of blood I can feel
I can experience through the Asanas

Blissfulness, satisfaction, all that I am feeling
through practising Asanas

The Mantra SO HAM I experienced through being
devotedly attached to the Asanas

Devotion I learned through the Asanas

Love I am feeling through the Asanas

That I am alive I enjoy feeling through the
Asanas

God I can feel through the Asanas

Thankfully I am practising Asanas

Everything I need to grow up spiritually I receive
through practising Asanas

Every cell is joyfully calling in me to do Asanas!

Asanas are the dance of divinity

Because you love

Because you love you are able to feel with me
Because you love you would never complain about
me
Because you love my poor English doesn't matter to
you
Because you love you will understand what I mean
when there are sometimes wrong words in
my poems
Because you love I will follow you
Because you love you are able to see the good side in
me too
Because you love you would never push me down
Because you love you are able to understand me
Because you love you will give me a hand
Because you love you are so proud of me
Because you love you will see the positive side in my
mistakes too
Because you love you are able to leave your ego
aside
Because you love you would never give me a lecture
Because you love you are able to listen to me too
Because you love you will sing for me about
Mahaprabhuji
Because you love you can see in me light, peace and
love
Because you love you are able to lift me up
Because you love I use every free minute to be with
you
Because you love you change the whole world into
heaven
Because you love others are like Angels for you

Ashram

There is one city: it is no different from the others. The houses are alike in every city. Only one house is different from the others. It has one thing special. From the outside you are not able to see it. Often, very often I passed it. I was suspecting nothing, knowing nothing of all the happiness, of all the love, of all the knowledge, of all the light and of the change of fate that can be possible inside.

This house, this special house has got a nightclub next-door. The duality is extremely close. In the one I am not interested at all, to the other I feel extremely attracted.

I am going step by step up the stairs, hoping and waiting for nothing and walking through the door, the door of luck, light, love and knowledge. Very slowly I realize that the longing, the thirst to find that superiority was within me. And I am not the only one of all the many people, who is going there with hope and longing to grow spiritually more and more. I can feel strongly, it is important to bring the light to others. To those, who are full of fear and with too many doubts.

I am very thankful, that I can carry the light and also that I know who kindled it within me.

I am happy that I am able to realize that without a Master I would be hopeless and I would, in my ignorance, fight to see the light.

Through Him I am able to see the light in Jesus, in Buddha, in Mahaprabhuji Deep. But only He could give that understanding und knowledge to me.

If you make your prayer, then think of the people who are without a Mantra and without guidance. Think of those who have to go alone to the light. And be thankful, if you have a spiritual guide.

Once there was

Once there was
A soul in a body
Locked up in it
Like in a cage

It had to pass through many actions
Until the first bar could break out of it

Still more had to happen for the next one
To break and even much more was necessary
To break the remaining ones

And it has to happen more and more
Until the soul will be able
To be released from karma and ignorance
Until the soul can again
Dissolve in the light to be free

Once it will be!
And then we will say

Once there was
A soul in a body
Locked up in it
Like in a cage

Once there was

The Domestic Gardener from Reichenau

Every day I run into two brown eyes. They belonged to an ascetic body who always seemed to be fully concentrated and who was radiating strength and unexpressed power. Something about him impressed me. I nodded to him kindly and much kindness and cordiality reflected back to me. This happened every day for the whole week.

On Friday Swamiji was sitting outside next to the tent. Many of us were sitting with him as usual. The gardener was working next to us. After some time he put his scythe on the ground and walked slowly towards our group, sat down keeping some distance between us. His eyes were resting on Swamiji, but after a while he went back to his work.

On Saturday, during breakfast, I saw him standing next to the buffet lost in his thoughts. For some seconds I saw a huge blue light around his head, not completely pure, but with a very large radiance. Now I know what was so fascinating for me about him.

Later we had a group photo. Again he came towards us: he liked to stand between us. He liked to belong to us. He was drawn to Swamiji like moths flying towards the light.

Retreat with Swamiji in Europe

That fate of the gardener has led him from his country to our country, from his home country to ours, to get the chance of his life to meet his Master. He himself didn't know it until that moment, why and what happened. But it was a must in his life, because by doing that he will be able to take his next step of the learning process in this life.

Everyone of us has the same experience, as the gardener and the moths, but many times we don't understand what is happening and therefore we don't always use our chance.

Once on a summer seminary the question appeared "how does the student get to his Master"? Swamiji answered at that time with a joke. But now I know the answer.

All of us are drawn to the light of the Master and also we are burning in his light. His light consumes our ignorance and karma.

Swamiji in India

Satsang

I am standing here and I am astonished and
I am looking and I am filled with love

I am standing here and
I don't know who I am

I am standing here and
I know that it is Christmas within me

A holy feeling is within me
Christmas is within me

Something in me wants to be born

Something in me is waking up

The same kind of feeling must be
In the flower buds before they bloom.

This holy feeling is spreading inside of me

I am silent, but I want to tell it to everyone
But inside of me there is fear
That by talking about it
I may losing it.

I love all of them
Because they are His Bhaktas

Then it is Him who raises me
When I have fallen

Then it is Him who catches me
When the wind blows me in the wrong direction

Then it is Him who holds me
When I sway

Then it is Him who strengthens me
When I am weak

Then it is Him who guides me
That I am able to realize God

I am standing here and I am astonished and
I am looking and I am filled with Love

I am standing here and I don't know who I am

I am standing here and
I know that Christmas is within me.

To Fly

What is it like to fly?
Will you be closer to the angels?
Will you feel sooner the vibrations of God?

What is it like to fly?
When the aeroplane is jetting through the air
And is pushing furrows there
Do angels make the furrows smooth again?
Are angels afraid to lose their wings?

What is it like when Swamis are flying?
Is the air resistance less?
Is the jet fuel cleaner?
Must then angels not be so busy?
Is the air then not so tense?
Will Prana – Cushions be softer there?

When you can see an aeroplane,
And you do not hear it,
Then Swamiji is on His journey
Very gently and softly
In His thoughts He is with us often
And He is sending to us His knowledge
And His Love.

I think, to fly without harming heaven
His Gurukripa only makes able
To travel like this.

ॐ

ओमकारं बिन्दु संयुक्तं नित्यं ध्यायन्ति योगिनः
कामदं मोक्षदं चैवं ओम काराय नमो नमः

omkāram bindu samyuktam nityam dhāyanti yoginaḥ
kāmadam mokṣadam caivam omkārāya namo namaḥ

OM

We are sitting closely together having coffee and cake, and we are trying to understand each other better. We would like to go together the spiritual path. We all have longing to know about God. We believe He is within us, but we have not yet experienced Him until now.

My friend is telling me about her meeting with others, when they pray the rosary together, when they take the spiritual path in company.

My question to her, do you sing OM before and afterwards?

My friend is extremely dismayed!

I try to explain to her how nice the vibration of the sound OM is. That out of the sound OM the world had risen and that the sound OM is connecting humans directly to God.

But she doesn't like to listen, she doesn't like to understand. She said the sound OM is an unknown energy and with this energy you can easily burn yourself.

But I'm thinking, if my mind is only concentrated on safety and if I don't want to risk singing OM to get closer to God. Why am I praying? Why do I long so much for Him and try to feel that I am one with Him? Will my friend really be one with Him? Is she really drawn so much towards Him? Is her fear much bigger than the longing for Him? Maybe she is right in her thinking. What if once I will burn myself? What if I will once run around with trimmed and burned wings?

What shall I do now? Who is ignorant? For some time I think in every direction, however I make my conclusion very easily.

I will definitely, with patience and a holy feeling go on singing OM until my last breathing. But my last breath shall be the sound OM.

Maybe the sound OM will burn me. But the OM-Ash will fly through the whole world and its holy vibration will take me everywhere, where people have learned to carry with the sound OM their longing for God.

Middle: His Holiness Mahamandaleshwar Paramhans Swami Maheshwarananda Puriji, called by His disciples Swamiji, He is my Guru.
Right: His Holiness Dharma Samrat Paramhans Swami Madhavananda Puriji, Swamijis Guru
Left: me

I am running

I am running, I am running
I am running behind Him
I am running, I am running
Trying to be in His footprints

I am running, I am running
I am exhausted, I am too slow
But still I am running and
I try to be with Him

I am running, I am running
He is my only aim
I am running, I am running
I would like to be with Him

I try to be quick and
I am running, I am running and
I do hope that my ego will not run with me

I am running, I am running
I know the time will come
When I am able to follow Him easily
But still I am running and
Only God knows when I will reach Him

I am wearing, I am wearing
I am wearing His dress
It was given time ago from Him to me
I am wearing His clothes and
I do hope it will burn my weaknesses
I am wearing His clothes and
I am too small for His width
I am trying to fit in
Only God knows when it will be

I am praying, I am praying
I am praying His prayers too
I am praying, I am praying
To reach God realisation
I am praying, I am praying to be in His heart
I am praying, I am praying
Let the divine knowledge rise
I am praying, I am praying
I am praying to be one with Him
And to be free like He is
So far I'm still within bonds
I am praying, I am praying but
Only God knows when it will be

At the same time I know
That I am He and
I know it, I know it
That He is me
I know it, I know it
That we are one and nothing can separate us
In order to realise this I was born.

Love

Do you know what Love looks like?
Do you know which kind of form Love has?
Do you know how the personified Love looks?
You can see Love not only with your inner eyes.
You are able to see Love in front of you.
You can touch Love,
If Love will allow you to do so.
This Love is here for you, only for you!
But at the same time it is for all,
For everyone and for every creature.
When I saw this Love personally
For the first time
Then I realized what Love is
Then I felt what Love means
Then I understood suddenly
It was so completely different from before
And again precisely the same as before
Do you know how Love looks like?
Do you know who Love is?
I will say only one word to you

Swamiji

His Holiness Jagadguru Vishwaguru Mahamandaleshwara Paramhansa Swami Maheshwarananda Puri Ji.

My Grandma was a very wise one

Berta Galler, my Grandma

I only saw her twice in my life
But she filled me with so much love
It will last at least for two lives

My grandma was a very wise on
She lost everything in her life twice
She managed to survive two wars
She was able to accept and not to be attached

My grandma was a very wise one
When her youngest son of 16 years
Was going to shoot people in the war
She prayed for him and she believed
That God will hear it

My grandma was a very wise one
I saw her when I was 4 and then 20 years later
She was the same one
She was filled with love

Her heart didn't want to beat any longer
But doctors treated her
And to her were given some more years

My grandma was a very wise one
She told me to every pot belongs a lid
She told me please wait till the right lid will fit
I was not able to wait and
I chose the wrong lid

My grandma was a very wise one
I was not patient and I chose twice
But only one was necessary
To fulfil my karma for this life

My grandma was a very wise on
She taught me to pray
She taught me to believe
That everything will come at the right time
Because the big puzzle of life has to fit

My grandma was a very wise one
She taught me that we have always
To decide by ourselves
She taught me that we are responsible
For our lives
She taught me just to give love
She taught me never to give up
She taught me just to "do good"

She taught me that luck is also waiting for me
She taught me to see the opposite side
She taught me to pray und believe

My grandma was a very wise one
She taught me to pray in the right way
Not to ask for anything
Not to wait for God to fulfil my wish
She taught me only to pray
For what has to happen will happen
For the benefit of others and also for me

My grandma was a very wise one
She taught me to be selfless
She taught me to just let it go and accept
To be patient and wait because
What will be will be

My grandma was a very wise one
She told me you can change countries
You can change continents
You can change your lives
But you cannot run away from your karma
Your destiny will run after you
You can never run quickly enough
It will find you and it will catch you

My grandma was a very wise one
She told me
Try to feel kindness always in your heart
For your friends, for animals, nature and God

Then God will bring you to the right shore
He will take care of you
And He will lead your life too

My grandma was a very wise one
I try to follow her teachings
And to live my life as it should be

With the grace of God it will not break my heart
With the grace of God I will manage everything
With the grace of God I will overcome difficulties
With the grace of God I will have patience
and love

With the grace of God
I also will be once a wise one

With the grace of God
Everything will be as it should be

Shower

It is such a great feeling to stand under the shower, to sprinkle oneself with soft warm water, to be worthy of soaping oneself to feel clean and fresh. And in the end to appreciate the joy of cold showering, to feel the cold water going under the skin, going through and through. But today I have overdone it. I was thoughtless. Not thinking of the fact that in Africa for example there is not enough water, that they have shortages of water and that there are many deserts on our earth. Everywhere are plants, animals and humans who are thirsty. Today I really squandered the water. The mirror in the bathroom was completely covered with steam. It looks like I am standing in fog. Only in the bottom the mirror is clean. I am able to see only my knees and feet.

Are the Asanas and Pranayama with whom I am practicing every day, able to clean the fog of ignorance that is still in me? To purify my karma? Is the fog that is hindering me to come quickly to God, to realize what is God? Is it now brighter around me already or am I still completely in ignorance?

Thanks to God through every fog the sun will be shining sometimes.

The daily shower is a quick cleaning of our body. It is also possible that there is a quick cleaning of our karma?

Why does the cleaning of the old karma slag and old karma waste need so much energy? Why does it need so much awareness? How does it happens that by going through so many incarnations there is still so much work to do, haven't those incarnations not been so good and positive?

Our past lives or our past deeds create so much fear in us, such huge fear that we nearly can't go on with our lives.

But God knows and gave us hope at our birth. Hope to improve everything in this life. This hope is a great gift for us, and it is the driving power to go on, trying to make things a little better every day. This hope will make sure that one day we are able to forget the paralysing fear that is within us.

This hope will help us to manage our life in a better way, in a spiritual way. This hope will let us realize that there is a longing within us to get back to our origin. And if we are aware of this longing it will appear within ourselves, the longing to receive Mantra from a self-realized Master, because our soul knows that without Mantra we will not be properly guided and protected on every level and we will again forget why we are here.

Our higher self also knows that receiving a Mantra from an enlightened Master is a quick shower to purify our Karma.

Imagine....

That you have the possibility of seeing Jesus! Would you go to see Him? Would you go through snow, slush, rain or heat, so that you are able to see HIM?

Imagine....

That you have the possibility of meeting the Holy Virgin Mary! Would you run there to get the blessing from HER?

Imagine.....

That you could meet a Saint! Would you believe that it could happen nowadays? Would you try to recognize HIM?

If you are honest with yourself, then you know that you would not go to Him. You would probably have a different destination.

Think what happened when Jesus was born. Only some people blew the horn, rejoiced that such immense Light came to earth. Only the three Holy Kings recognized it and went towards Him immediately.

The others were very much in doubt, perhaps were very preoccupied in their minds. Their minds were running here and there. They were not able to agree with their conscience, they preferred to continue as before at their homes and they were not able to see in the little child, the Light, Jesus Christ. Everything else was more important for them, everything, except going to the LIGHT!

If you have a longing to grow in the direction to the Light and seriously show effort, everything will come by itself. You only need to feel the strong desire within yourself.

When your longing to see the Light break through, you can no longer ignore it. Then you will look for a Saint who speaks to you. Be sure, you will recognize the Light in Him and He will be your guide forever.

You don't need to look around you any more and wander about. Nothing more will be able to stop you.

You are suddenly completely sure
You are suddenly completely free

You will fulfil your daily duties with much more Love and Joy and you will feel within your-self so much happiness too. Nobody and nothing will hold you back anymore. Nothing will be able to keep you from striving towards the Light.

Imagine.....
How nice would it be if the Light within your-self flared up and you were completely filled with it. It would take darkness and ignorance from you.

Imagine.....
That you were standing in the middle of Light!

Imagine.....

You would be shining and glowing and would be perfectly pure.

Then being a beacon could be a duty for you too.

Longing

What is it that is crying in me?
What is it that is sobbing in me?

What wants to be happy in me? Am I crazy? Am I depressed? Are there not millions like me? What am I? What would I like to be and how would I like to be? Am I addicted? Is everything in me only superficial? Does it melt away before I can observe it? What is it that torments me? What is it that makes me struggle? I don't know! What are others doing so that they are so joyfully wandering through life? I would also like to be in Ananda and in Bliss. I absolutely know that I am also guided and led. But why am I not able to feel it?

Longing consumes me. I have the feeling I am like a thirsty fish outside the water. I know within me is Divine Light! But why don't I see and feel it!

I want to be pure, very simple and only be His. Within me there should only be Light, Divine Knowledge and Love. I am desperate because I have to wait; I am desperate although I know that it will come about!

I so much want to be completely pure and to be only be His. I was begging for that, "Please, Lord take that strong painful longing away from me that I want to be pure and that I want to be only with YOU"! But He knew it so much better than I, and He gave to me much more pain.

Now I thank Him every day for that feeling, that strong longing for Him in my heart. Today I know it is the most precious gift I got from Him on my path.

However I wish to be pure, at all levels, and just to be His. I wish to be pure, completely pure. That is why I now beg You my Lord, please help me to walk my path, please help me to see the Light. Please take away the darkness from me and lift the veil of ignorance for me.

It is more and more clear to me, how much I do need YOU !

I am so sad

I am so sad because I am not able to help
I passed the shop and what did I see?
A picture on the newspapers front side
A picture where an old woman was crying!

This woman in tears
In her heart I could see her pain
The pain so endless, so strong and so deep
Who causes someone to cry like this?

This human being made very bad karma
And karma like that
Will come back, and not only this
Also the pain I felt about her
So deep in my heart
It also will come back to the person
Who created it

And not only did I feel
That strong pain of the woman
I am sure all who saw that picture felt it
Now you know which pain will come back
To that person who caused the woman to cry

It's a picture from the war
Now in the year 2002.
This Karma will come back,
It will come back to that person
It might come very soon
Or maybe later in another life

But it will come
The Cosmic Law is the same for everyone

I am preparing a Saint's visit
In a small city at the moment
Swamiji will come
Giving lectures about World Peace

How to get and to keep the World Peace?

He has tried all His life
To awaken human awareness
To live and practice Ahimsa, the non-violence,
For that He is working 24 hours day by day

How sad for all of us
That some people are not able to keep peace
That they are not able to keep peace
Within their families

That they are not able
To keep peace with their friends
That they are not able
To keep peace within their countries

And they are giving the order to shoot
To shoot others
And they are not able to feel their pain
They are not able to renounce
And to give up pollution of mind

They don't know that happiness
Is in renunciation and in giving up!

Let us try together, again and again
To feel peace in our hearts

Let us give up greediness
Let us give Love to all creatures

Love unites and Love purifies

Let us try to be wholly conscious all the time
Let us beg for forgiveness
For all the pain we have brought about
Let as try to become
Better and better human beings

It is only this we should never give up!

Spiritual Step Number One

The Guru was given two scarves for a present
And He thought...
"What should I do with the two of them?
I cannot use everything by myself
But I cannot give them away for a present
They are of tough fibre
Nobody will be happy with this gift"!

He puts the two scarves in a drawer
So that they will soften each other
Now they just lie and wait there,
And after some weeks He needs a present,
That's why He thinks of them.
After all, how are they now?
Still, neither will make anyone happy yet.

Resolutely He makes them soft
Beating one scarf with the other,
And He is amazed
To see some good qualities in them.

He is surprised to see this!
But all of us know;
The Love from Him to us
Makes a swan out of a crow and
Leads us from fear to Love

The Guru shakes the dust
From His divine hands
And He turns to events
Which do have much more importance!

The Rose

Our holiday was over. It was raining very hard. The weather was tempting us to be lazy; it was perfectly suited for taking a rest. Every day it was raining very strongly, nearly all day long.

We went to take the last breakfast of this holiday. In the breakfast hall they had put a beautiful rose on every table. One of those roses was a very special one. It was standing at the neighbour's table. Nobody was sitting there. There were no dishes, only a clean tablecloth and on top of it this beautiful rose. I was not able just to pass by; not only my hands embraced it very carefully, also I brought my face close to it. The wonderful scent remained on me. During breakfast I constantly had to look at the rose. I completely soaked up its messages like a sponge.

We had to leave this lovely holiday place and say goodbye to everybody. The parting was this times an especially cordial one. Travelling home was a smooth affair; there was not much traffic on the road. While travelling, I was beholding the rose. It accompanied me. It had made a very strong impression on me. What does it want to say to me?

The rose was completely open. The petals were fully fanned out. The rose showed its tenderness. It showed all its sensitivity and its beauty. It showed its trust that what ever would happen, would be good for it.

This certainty is what we would call self-confidence, an unconditional opening, a kind of surrender to our creator. I was deeply impressed.

Never before had I got such an intense message from another creature. And never before had I been so sensitive and open that I could feel this so immensely strongly.

Please God make me able to open myself up so completely and unconditionally to YOU as that rose does.

My First Trip to INDIA

India, the heart of the world, as people call it, is really a special country. You can find every kind of climate and weather, desert as well as fully green areas, forests, hills, all kinds of nature. Of course there are very large rivers too. In India you will find everything you are searching for. If your eyes are only open for worldly things, you will see only those, for instance poor people with very little money or extremely rich people with a lot of it. Many people have not got what we think to be the level of mere existence. Mostly they are happy, because of a different kind of thinking and their knowledge of a COSMIC LAW.

You will be able to see beautiful things, like buildings, nature, animals etc. You are a lucky person when you are able to open the eyes of your heart. India is a holy country. You can feel a different kind of vibration immediately when you arrive. You will always find holy people there. The fine, spiritual vibration, the radiance from the holy people is one of the reasons why our world is not collapsing but still functioning somehow and nature surrounding us is not more diseased now. Believe me plants are suffering very much because of our carelessness. Nevertheless, all this really was not the reason I was travelling to India.

I was really lucky to meet two holy persons. I saw it as a blessing from God not only to see them, but also to sit next to them and listen to them. I had been dreaming of this ever since my childhood. Through their protection I haven't any illness and I have always felt like being in heaven.

Holy Guruji and Swamiji

True, I have seen extremely poor people in India. In the beginning I felt pain in my heart. However, some time later I realized that you can call really poor only those people who live without thinking of God. People who are not honest and kind, not helpful to other creatures, animals, plants, human beings and don't protect any kind of creatures, those people lend really poor lives.

Real poverty is when you are frozen in your feelings, without love in your heart.

God loves every one of His children. Animals and plants are his children too. He loves everyone, whether they are perfect in their deeds or not. For Him it doesn't matter if the body is perfect and beautiful, well built or crippled. And whether we are thinking of Him or not, He is always with us.

We shouldn't say; "Oh, I have so many sorrows, so many painful matters around me, God is not thinking about me, He has forgotten me". Some people say God does not exist at all. Some say nobody has seen Him, I cannot touch Him either. But there are also many people who have experienced Him. What about these people? To me it is like people in Austria saying: "the ocean does not exist at all, because I cannot see it". Austrian people live in the middle of Europe, in the heart of Europe. Around this country there is only land, huge hills and beautiful valleys. The ocean is very far away. Many people never have seen it, not once in their life, because to travel there is very expensive. But the ocean exists whether you believe it or not. The same is true about God.

What harms us in our lives are the deeds of our former lives. Everything we now do, think und speak will come back to us. That is a cosmic law. Good deeds or bad deeds, it doesn't matter, will come back to us. We are harming ourselves or making ourselves happy. Every action provokes a reaction. God is the one who always forgives us everything. He is the one who always loves us. It doesn't matter what kind of character we have. The love of God for His children is endless. Sometimes we just forget that the plants and animals are His children too. I always felt this so strongly and I knew I would find out more about this in India.

But back to what the journey meant to me. It was my first time in India. It was also the first time I travelled alone. Before, I had always been travelling with family members. I was extremely afraid of any type of journey. I was afraid from one of going suburb to the other. This journey was something very special for me I was brave enough, to travel without my family. I travelled by myself and was completely surprised not to feel any kind of fear. When I was sitting in the aeroplane, I could not believe it! I was very carefully listening to myself, but I felt only joy. What had happened? What and why was that gigantic change within me?

How amazing it was for me! I could not believe that the woman next to me was crying, completely nervous of even sitting in a plane. She was exhausted after a short time, how would it be in a few more hours? She was extremely afraid of this long flight. So many hours just sitting in the air, only to think about this, troubled her so much. She could not enjoy the flight, and I could not understand her, because I had already forgotten how I had felt before. Before, I had felt just like her, being afraid during the flight.

When we came to New Delhi it was very humid. It was about +30 degrees in the middle of the night and we where coming directly from winter. At home it was very cold at that time, many degrees below Zero. Some people from the Ashram in Jaipur picked us up, and we travelled together to Jaipur during the night.

In India there is left-hand driving, but people usually drive in the middle of the road directly confronting each other. They only move to the side a few metres before they are about to collide. Really, at the last moment they move to the right or left side, it depends in which direction they go. For me it was terrible to see that. Still, I was so fascinated with this way of using the road that I was not able to look at anything else. Also the horns are being blown constantly. Toot, toot, and toot everywhere, such an enormous noise. I am sure nobody knew to whom this hooting was addressed, and no one knew why, it was completely chaotic. I could not believe this could work. The roads are also somehow very strange. To me it looked as if the workers had just poured some buckets of tar on the ground, which means on the sand, and let the tar just flow. There in Rajasthan there is almost only sand. The soil is very poor. Building roads is very difficult in this area. The sand is so volatile and it is very difficult to keep the roads in place there. Now I know why it is a very hard task to build roads in Rajasthan. But at that time I didn't have much knowledge about India.

Slowly after some time on the road, I started to see other curious things. For example motels and bus stops. All of us had to go to the toilet, but we could see from one toilet into the other and we could not believe that there were

only holes in the floor and there was no paper anywhere! We were horrified! Now I am laughing about that, but at that time I didn't know how to deal with it and all important thoughts about hygiene were on my mind. Everything that I am telling you now had happened years ago, between the first trip and today. After this journey I stayed in India for a few years and I could experience how the Indian toilets function. Now I know it is the most economical and hygienic way to use that special place.

Before we arrived in Jaipur the sun was rising and turned the yellow sand totally pink. It was beautiful beyond description and I will never forget it.

When we entered Jaipur elephants were crossing the road and on the side of the street there were even more. The elephants were carrying wood. My heart was jumping for joy to see the elephants. Never before had I seen elephants walking freely in the street. I had seen them only in zoos! When freely walking between houses and people you realize how gigantic they are, how great they are! They radiated to me so much love and knowledge from thousands of years. I could immediately feel that we were in love with each other. All this happens only within seconds. We could look each other into the eyes only for one moment, but it was enough for all of us to realize and suddenly to know that we are in reality one.

Every time I returned to Jaipur, or when I left Jaipur or India, the elephants were standing or walking in the streets. For me it was a sign that I was moving on the right spiritual path, for me an extremely good sign. There were forty other people in the bus, but I was the only one who made this experience with the elephants. They had already been my favourite animals when I was a baby.

Sometimes elephants came into the city, when there was a big festival like a wedding ceremony. Then appeared elephants beautifully coloured and painted, I had the good fortune to see them in these ceremonies.

I could touch them, and I was surprised how soft their skin was. To feel the warmth of the trunk, to feel how sensitive their nostrils are, and to observe that they could feel my touching their trunk. It was amazing to see that such a huge animal has a way of looking at you like a little innocent baby and is waiting to see if there is love coming from your heart towards him. I know I am forever in his heart. When I left the elephant looked sad and I was sad too.

We stayed in Jaipur for some days, and we relaxed and enjoyed being there. When we went sightseeing in the city it was very interesting for me too. We bought some presents for our friends and visited some museums and some temples. There were always so many beggars at

these places, which was very disturbing for us. We never knew to whom we should give money and to whom we shouldn't. At such places begging is mostly organised and they don't really need the money. However maybe there were some among them who were not organized, but we decided to give nothing more at such places. If you give, you are never able to give to everyone. Also I remembered the words of my Master, he once said: "Don't give money, give knowledge, because only knowledge can really help them". But everyone among us had an extremely bad feeling about this. We felt it was most difficult to deal with this matter.

In Jaipur there is a famous school for astrology. On the outside of the building they have chiselled the whole universe in stone. The school has been known for hundreds of years throughout the whole world. There is built in the right proportions, the earth to the sun, the moon, and the stars and in which direction they are wandering, what distance, how long between one point und the other. All this is chiselled in stone. It is amazing to see the relationship between them. You can see there much you would like to know about astrology.

The most fascinating thing I saw were the monkeys. Jaipur is a very big city. In this huge city, there are still living wild monkeys, a gigantic number of them. Sometimes they can be dangerous, especially when they don't get what they want. You never know what the monkey will take away from you. Maybe he will take your glasses or your handbag with your passport and money? Maybe he only likes to sit on your shoulder because it is so funny. We could see monkeys climbing through windows, stealing something interesting to them, and then they just put it into another window which maybe belongs to a different family. We saw a man scolding the animal from the street but the monkey only enjoyed it, it didn't bother him at all. Monkeys are used staying in the city. They are strong and look very healthy.

After some days of rest we continued travelling to the Kailash Ashram. Kailash Ashram is situated in a very small village in Rajasthan. The Ashram is approximately about 200 metres off the main street. The bus couldn't go there because the sand is so fine that the wheels would sink deeply into it as if it were deep, freshly powdered snow. So we had to walk with our luggage the short distance to the Ashram. It was a big adventure for us. We were terribly afraid of snakes and scorpions. This was not a good feeling at all. We were sinking in, walking one step forward and two steps backward. Some Indians were looking at us and laughing. They are used walking in the sand and make it look easy.

The Ashram in Kailash is a very powerful one, situated in a powerful place. The vibration here is so strong that even people who do not have any experience with this are able to feel it. In this Ashram Paramyogeshwar Shri Devpuriji had been living for some years.

Ashram in Kailash

Shri Devpuriji had some Siddhis. For example He preferred to ride on a white horse when He was going to Satsang. People could not see Him. They could only see the horse. When Shri Devpuriji climbed down He let people see Him. People in this area already knew this, but they were always surprised again. For me this was a special moment in my life, when people talked about Him. Many people here are still alive who saw Him, knew Him and spoke to Him personally. Shri Devpuriji passed away in 1942. When a yogi dies it is called Mahasamadhi.

Shri Devpuriji

After Kailash Ashram we travelled to Khatu Ashram, the Shri Deva Dungary Samnyasi Ashram. Khatu is far away from civilisation. It is a very special place as well. In Khatu there is almost no water. When staying there, you have to think very carefully about the use of water and not to waste it. If you want to have water for cooking, then you will not have water to wash yourself. If you want to wash yourself, at least a little, then you may not have enough water to wash your bottom when you need to (Indians using water and not paper. They always have water with them). Do not think there is enough water for washing your dishes. Your plate you have to clean with sand, like I saw it when I was in Africa. The sand will take away the oily film on your plate and you will be surprised how clean it will be. Still it is very strange for us foreigners. When you have to go to the toilet, you have to look far a place where you can hide yourself. We people from the West are not used to sit in the open where everybody can watch us. Indians in that area are used doing it in that way and they are not shy about it. White people come to this area very, very rarely and it was a sensation for people who lived there to see white people. The nearest houses are about half an hour away from this Ashram. The next village is far, about one hour's walk.

In Khatu there was living the holy man Mahaprabhuji Deep. He went in Mahasamadhi 1963 at the age of 135 years. At that time I was a young girl and where I lived no special spiritual education would have attracted me. If somebody had asked me, "would you like to go on the spiritual path"? I would probably have thought, "What does he or she mean"? But in fact spirituality was part of my life, only I was not aware of it.

When I was in Khatu I realized all those things. I realized that the holiest man, of this

Bhagawan Sri Deep Narajan Mahaprahuji

distance place, had been protecting and guiding me all my life. Many times I just did not understand and sometimes I was running in the wrong direction. But He always took me back on the right path.

The Khatu Ashram is such a strong and holy place: you can still feel the presence of the Saint Mahaprabhuji Deep.

People from that area say, there were raining flowers from the sky when He was born. The fine vibration around people speaking about Him is simply indescribable.

At this place, Khatu Ashram there is nothing comfortable about, only sand, stones, thorns, camels and wild dogs.

The dogs are very dangerous at night, because they are hunting for food. Many people there simply have not what they really need for themselves, so they are not able to feed dogs. At day time normally you can touch the dogs and they will enjoy it. But at night they will forget that you have caressed them before and they might attack you. Camels can be very dangerous here as well. Camels in Rajasthan are working animals and they work extremely hard. Not all of them are well treated by their owners. Therefore some of them don't trust people.

There was a very big Satsang to welcome us. Hundreds of people came to listen to our Master's lecture, to enjoy being at the Satsang, to see the people from the west, to welcome us. Some people came by camel. It looked beautiful when they were sitting on camels. The women are very colourfully dressed in their saris and the men mostly wear white Dhotis and Kurtas. Camels walking in sand make a crunchy sound as if it was snow when it is very, very cold. I was lying in the tent and listening to this sound long before I could see them. It was like being in a fairy tale. It was so uncanny that I thought I was dreaming. The moon was full and it was quite light outside.

To these guests at the Satsang we didn't look well educated, because we were not able to eat with our fingers in the proper way. We asked for a spoon. We did not know how to sit on the floor. We did not have the right experience or knowledge how to drink in the right way: we touched the metal cups with our lips. What a shame for us! But they were very patient and were trying to teach us how to eat, to drink and other things. They must have thought our behaviour to be hopeless. Most of them had never before seen any people from the West.

The turning of the Year from 1990 to 1991 we celebrated in Khatu. In this night, the full moon was standing on the horizon at midnight on one side, and on the opposite there was still standing the sun. It was a special constellation in this night. Swamiji said it would bring good luck, and those who were taking the spiritual path seriously might reach self-realization in this life.

After some days in Khatu we continued to travel to Bola Guda. Bola Guda is also a very

Bhagawan Sri Deep Narajan Mahaprabhuji

powerful place where the Holy Man from Khatu, Mahaprabhuji Deep stayed every once in a while.

Bola Guda is far inside the desert. The sand is finer; it is extremely fine, so that sometimes you cannot breathe. We were really thankful when there was no wind. But when the Wind had decreased the heat was so terrible, we could not breathe because of the hot air. The problem with water was much more intense. We had to wait a long time for a little water, because the wells could not give us as much as we would have liken to have.

We people from the West are really spoilt. We have so much water that nobody ever thinks about saving it. The animals in this area are very badly off as well. They drink water from everywhere no matter what it looks or smells like. In this area people like to have water buffalos because they can stand heat and sun better. Water buffalos like to lie in the water ponds and they are so lazy that they do not need to drink much. And still they give more milk than cows. Milk from a water buffalo tastes very oily and greasy. Indians mostly like to mix buffalo milk with cow's milk and water.

Cows in India are holy animals. India's cows are special. Cows here are mainly light grey and thin. When I saw a wild cow for the first time, I thought it was a stag. But they told us there are still wild cows in Rajasthan. They look like stags. The brown colour of their coat is slightly reddish. They are able to jump over walls.

But back again to the village Bola Guda. At the Ashram there lives a Swami. It is my ideal to stay at such a holy place. I don't know if I would always feel this fine spiritual vibration. Maybe I would get used to it and no longer feel it any more.

To live in an extremely simple way would help to be directed solely towards God.

Travelling through India and visiting those places makes us aware of the meaning of our life and of our duties in this life. If we are in extreme situations, then we become aware of something because our mind is only concentrated on one thing, in other words we are empty. We can look into ourselves, and know the truth.

But why do we forget so quickly what is within ourselves, and which we would like to work on?

The orange flag shows that it is a Samnyasi Ashram

Rescue

There is no shouting for help
There is no wish to get help
But you know if you do not help,
Somebody will drown.

You can see it,
You can see it precisely,
Everybody can see it,
But only one is jumping into the water
Which is as cold as ice
To hold out the hand
To the drowning person

It is not about asking,
It is about knowing.

The person fights back
Refuses to accept the proffered help.
Fights back with his mind,
Feet and hands
But the rescuer, his Guru,
Grips him and pulls him
On the bank firmly.

It is not about asking,
It is about knowing.

The Guru goes forward,
It is not about asking,
It is about knowing,
And takes care of the other person again.

The Master knows about our karma,
He knows about our weaknesses,
And again and again
He tries to get us out
Of darkness and into the light.

He has been trying to save us
Already in many, many lives.

You have only one person
Whom you can really trust.
Your Master will never cheat you
He will always love you,
Will always help and protect and forgive you.

What is Mantra to us?

Mantra is kindling on the divine light within you.

Mantra belongs to the things, which we would be searching for, if they did not already exist,

Mantra is like the bush knife for the jungle,
Mantra is like going over a bridge,
Mantra is a labourer from God,
Mantra is like rain in the drought,
Mantra is a stop-gap to hunger,
Mantra is the power station within us
Mantra helps us to persist in the longing for God
Mantra is like you had wings
Mantra will help you to be very close to your protection angels and God

Mantra is like listening how the grass is growing
Mantra makes you invulnerable
Mantra is like listening to everlasting sounds of God
Mantra multiplies Love

With Mantra the whole world will suddenly open for you. You can feel that plants and animals are hoping for your protection, and you know that you are responsible for them too.

Through Mantra you know how to look after nature and preserve it. You will only want to eat fruit and grain and no meat! And you are resolved not to squander.

Mantra is helping you to live life as a true human being.

With Mantra you will not be lost in the universe and when born again, you will be in the hands of the Lord.

If you still don't know what Mantra is like, then pray to God and with His help you will find the Light.

Holy Guruji, practicing Mantra-Japa

Shraddha (confidence)

You are wearing Orange,
The colour of hope, of love, of delight.

You are wearing Orange
The colour of happiness

You are wearing Orange
The colour of surrender

You are wearing Orange
The colour for reaching eternal life

You are wearing Orange
The colour of being forever

But, having so much fortune
You have forgotten one thing
You cannot hide yourself anymore
You can no longer go anywhere
Just secretly to cry

All, all belongs only to Him
Your thoughts, your joy
Your knowledge and your being

When the others would let you just die
Only He will forever give you His hand
He will never leave you alone
He will give to you everything you need
We just have to learn to give everything to Him

That’s why just let it flow
And let it come and let it go
Take your time
And he will let you understand

You have got time, as much as you need
We have got many lives
To find out more
But be careful
And do not waste this life

God will carry you as soon the time is ripe
To your next learning process and
He will guide your life

You have to do only one thing
Waiting and calling Him again and again
For that you have got your Mantra

And if you give everything to Him
Then the darkness within yourself
Will not remain
And you will gain the Divine Light from Him

Your Meditations Place –
The Island of Happiness

I have found it
It is very difficult to find
You have to search
To search very intensely
And when you have found it
Then it belongs to you forever
It had taken a long time until I found it
I needed nearly half a century

This Island is in the middle of the ocean of peace
To this Island belongs the highest hill of Love
The wild animals become completely tame here
From this Island you can see every star
Every continent
Every village and every city too
You are able to see every plant from here
And every creature

The nicest sounds
The most beautiful colours are at home here
Nowhere else is it as exciting, as joyful as here

On this Island you can feel especially strong
Your Master is carrying you towards your aim
The only thing you need on this Island is Trust
And you can feel that you are at one with Him
You know that everything is within you
You don't need anymore to look
At different places to find HIM

Sometimes animals do have their wild days
Then Mahaprabhuji holds them back
And you will not fall into Maya's net

Vishwa Deep Gurukul:
Vill. Jadan, Distr. Pali, Rajasthan/ India

When the hurricane sweep over the Island
Then your Master will protect you and help
That you are able to keep yourself in peace

And slowly, step by step,
Through His help and His guidance
You will be able to become self-realization.

Hidden Beauty at Jadan

The Watermelon Angel

I'm sent into the world
And I don't know why
There are questions and questions
It will never end
Until I have found the reason

I am asking myself
Why do I only use the word NO?
Someone will help me and I just say NO
Someone likes to present me precious gifts
Someone will lift me up
And I am listening to myself
Again saying NO

Sometimes I was deeply wishing
That I could get some help
Sometimes I was asking
Sometimes I was crying
Sometimes I was praying to God; please help!

The helpers were coming
The help was there
But I could not accept it
It was offered to me, and again I said NO

I always asked myself
Why the NO is coming so fast.
Why the NO is coming so spontaneously
The NO was always quicker than the YES
This question has existed in my whole life

My hair became grey
But still I have not found the answer up to now
And I was asking myself
Asking and asking again and again
What is it that's wrong with the NO and the YES?

I am hungry
I just should go and buy something but what?
I don't want cheese
I don't want meat, I don't want rice
I don't know what I would like
I am only hungry for Prana, the energy of life
But then I decide to buy a watermelon

I try to cut it, but it has got a very hard skin
I try to cut it, but I am not able
To put the knife in its skin

Next to me an angel is standing and asks me
Shall I cut it for you?

Surprise! Now a YES comes from me

He cuts the melon in an especially nice way
And puts the nice pieces on a separate plate
Those which are less good are put aside

I am talking and looking at the angel's cutting
"The plate with the nice pieces"
He said, "these are for you "

We are eating, we are talking
I can feel that the angel's heart is hurting too

I think I am full up and I can not take more pain
I cannot take more suffering
I cannot take the slightest bit more
My own heart has such deep wounds
I am no more able to deal with this!
I am overloaded and I have enough
Of everything!

But suddenly
I am able to understand many things!
Suddenly I am able to understand
How everything is linked!

Now I am able to understand my NO!
Now I am able to say YES!

I have been waiting for that since my childhood
I have been waiting and now I know!
I have been waiting and waiting for that moment
Very long time

My new awareness makes me patient!
That is what makes me meek!

It is the selfless gift from others to me!
This is why my YES was coming
This is why I am now able to accept

Now I am able to understand
Why the YES could not be voiced until now

And we can see how important unselfishness is
The Angel was not waiting for something

There only was LOVE
There was just the wish for giving
The wish to understand and to help
The Angle will be in my heart and prayers forever

Towards God there is only one extremely small path. On it we have to go alone towards the Light. We are not able to walk with pride either. We can walk on it only with selflessness and love.

Noting will be easier as this if we have passed process of life's purification.

The Cuddle

The mother brings her child to Him and you can observe cuddling is giving everything and giving all the love that's within

That is giving in great abundance. It is showing the abundance of Love to you. It happens in an abundance of purity. You are hardly equal to this. You are feeling the unity just through watching this

You are getting so much but you would like to give from yourself too and you can feel in this cuddling is the blessing of God.

This cuddling is able to make everything swing. You feel how they join in purity and around them is to be seen a great transformation.

My Mother with me

Around them are only clarity, love and sonorous swinging. This is a holy moment for you too. It is able to make stones and plants sing and you can feel when all actions were so pure and full of this unconditional Love there wouldn't be wars anywhere. There wouldn't be misunderstandings; People all would live in harmony with each other. Everybody would wish his neighbours the best. Nature would recover much more quickly.

We would be able again to pick the stars from the sky for our friends. We would be able again to move mountains for them as if it was easy.

We would be able again to feel that everything is within us like the stars, the Divine Light, Bliss and Love.

We would know again that we receive much more than we are ever able to give.

We would more easily leave this world. We would leave it without fear. We would remember again our human duty and our divine aim. We would be able to realize all about God.

Also we could give more Light, Love and Wisdom to others. From ourselves can only come what is within us.

That's why you ought to
Open quickly your heart.

Open yourself
And let flow the abundance
Of light and love
The great gift from God to us
Through cuddling,
Through words,
Through glances and glimpses,
Through your being
And through your deeds

Then the circle can be closed again, everything is given to us by God

Everything that comes from the heart will flow back to the Divine Source, to God, where everything begins

The Wheat

I am not a farmer, I am not a country man, and I am not a rancher. I do not even have a small garden! Nothing belongs to me! Nevertheless, Mother Nature gave to me a phenomenal, an enormous present. A present that, I am sure, very few people will get. I think it was a great fortune to receive knowledge about that special moment, as it is great luck to recognize a Master.

We were living in a big city and we went to the countryside to spend some days to recover and have a rest. We wanted to pamper ourselves with a lot of fresh air, healthy food, more activity and enough sleep. The weather was just perfect for this kind of holiday. The days were sunny and the nights were fresh and cool. We had also taken our bicycles with us. Every day we rode into the countryside, over the hills and into the valleys. It was so beautiful.

On one of those days, I was riding to get to be ahead of Hans. He wanted to shoot a film of me. So I kicked a part of the hill, I sat on a bench for a short time and wanted to inhale in me all the beauty, all the magnificence that was around me, before I rode back. I was in a special state. I was completely satisfied and in harmony with everything around me.

Suddenly there was a cracking sound, very soft but on the other hand very loud, close to me. For one moment everything was completely soundless. Even butterflies and birds remained silent and without movement.

I felt it was a great, a holy moment. The whole atmosphere was filled with a special energy. Suddenly this cracking sound started again and continued. One seed of the wheat told it to the other. There were billions and I had a feeling I was able to listen to every grain separately. Although the tremendous openings within the wheat created billions of cracking sounds, there was an infinite stillness in the air. No birds were singing any more, not one cricket was chirping, and every creature was eavesdropping me like full of devotion for this holy moment. Every being around me, every blade of grass, every flower, and every earth-crumb knew; now the wheat is ripe.

I don't know if it wasn't already too late to harvest the grain when the grain would already fall out of its cover during the cutting and not just by threshing. Maybe the farmer had been late for harvesting the wheat. But for this wheat it was the right moment for its opening.

In one part of the Guru Gita it says; "please let my light in the heart catch fire from yours". That reminds me of the first seed cracking open. It also reminds me of meditation, where also the smallest light can suddenly flare up, if He is with us, He who can give that power to us.

What am I?
Why am I?
Why am I as I am?

I know only some people here
But these are the perfect ones.

You can look at them from every side and you will just find that they are very nice

It is very easy to respect and to love what is perfect
It is very easy to love people who are without any faults

What I am
That I am blessed to be with them?
What I am
That I have that great fortune to be with them?

I am nothing
I am less than that

I am just someone who makes everything not only bad but worse!
So some of the nice people keep complaining about me!

I have to change my prayer and I will do it quickly!

Until now I prayed: Mahaprabhuji Deep may I ask you let every thought
Let every deed
Let every word from me be just as you would like it to be.
Please let me be your channel for light, knowledge, love and peace.
Please let me be as YOU think that I am right, that I should be.

From now on I will pray: Mahaprabhuji Deep please let me be as others would like me to be, just for keeping the peace.

But Mahaprabhuji
This kind of prayer does not feel right for me.
I think I will go on and pray that I should be in that way YOU would like me to be.
I am sure the time will come and people will like to be with me.
I know it, it will come!

But until now people keep saying I am not the right one.

They think that I am not good enough for them.
I should do the whole lot by myself.
And of course especially
What others don't like to do
For that I am good for, but only for that!

Also they think I should listen only to their advice
And not to my spiritual guidance!

I do hope for the others
That they will once get their dream guide
But I think until then
I have managed to be self-realized

Swamiji at Barcelona

Why singing Bhajans about HIM?

Some nice devotional songs would be just as good
God is within everything
It doesn't matter in which language
It doesn't matter which soul will sing

My experiences are different
I know that singing is opening the heart
I know that singing is bringing us towards love
I know that every religion and every devotional song about God is a good one
I know also like you do and that I love God

Because I know
Who is carrying me towards the light

Because I know
Who is taking care of me so that I am not afraid

Because I know
That is the reason why I would like to sing Bhajans only about Him and for Him

Because I know
That I am not able to sit comfortably between two chairs

Because I know

If I call every minute for a different Saint none will come and no light will be sent

Because

Before the Saint is settled within me I will already call the next one and again I am not able to catch light, peace, knowledge and love from Him

I am happy to be settled in the light. Now I am able to see there is only One and it doesn't matter how I call Him

But the strongest ray of light I received only through concentration on one

So we have to decide to be with one

So we have to decide which saint should teach us to carry on

So we have to decide by ourselves what we want

If you are in a church which belongs to Jesus then you will be singing about him

If you are in a Mosque and you visit Allah then you will bring your devotion to him

If you are in a Shiva Mandir then you will bow down to him my dear

If you are in the Ashram from Mahaprabhuji Deep then you will show your respect to him

It shows that you do respect God in every form

It shows that you have achieved some knowledge until now

I will try to explain better

If you are in love with someone then you have your love in your heart for 24 hours a day

It doesn't matter what you are doing

It doesn't matter on what you are concentrating

It will fill you completely and you will have longing to be with your love

In your mind and in your heart will be only the name of your love

It will sing in you all day and all night

That vibration will call your love to come towards you and your love will have the longing to stay all the time with you

If it arises in you to sing Bhajans about Mahaprabhuji Deep it will complete your devotion to him

It shows that you are a devotee to Him and you will slowly become one with Him

To become one with a Saint, with your spiritual guide
Means to reach God-realization
Means that you will forever be free

Please let me stay alive

For you I am only a lobster, a cold-blooded animal and only an animal. You think I don't feel pain. But it is not true. I only cannot scream like you. I can only show you all my discomfort, my fear, my horror and my dismay through my wriggling and fidgeting. But this you don't want to see. This you dislike and refuse to admit. But I would truly like to stay alive.

You are horrified about cannibals because people are eating people. For me you are a cannibal too.

You have already forgotten that it was God who has also created me. You should protect and preserve us animals and not murder us. What would you like to do with me, what do you intend? To kill and eat me is simply murder.

It is cruel to be thrown into boiling water. Only people who do not care will be able to do so. Only people who don't have feeling for animals can do this and can eat us.

How do you feel when you eat me? How do you feel digesting my flesh, my fear and my dismay? How do you feel if I lie in your stomach?

Is it troubling your soul? Why are you interfering with the course of my life? You have got enough opportunities for eating. Why do you like eating corpses?

Ducks on the way towards the light

Would you like to know how God smells?

So just rub a little bit on a fir needle
And sniff it, and then you know
That only God is able to smell like this

Stroll along the beach
Inhale the smell of saltwater
And seaweed very deeply
And you suddenly know
Only God can be so fragrant so pure
And so clean like that

Press your face into the grass
Do it very gently and very softly
And you know that only God
Can smell so incomparable like that

Do you smell the flowers?
Each, yes each smells so differently, and so fine
So only God can smell
So captivating and so pure

Do you like to listen to God?
Just eavesdrop on the rain
So soft and gentle
So loud and so heavily drumming down
So only God is able to do it

Eavesdrop on the snowflake
On the butterfly's flight
Flying so soundless like this
Can only be the ONE

Listen to the wild brook
Listen to its babbling
Listen to the rush of the sea
This kind of sound
This only has got HE

Would you like God to touch you?
Would you like to feel HIM?
Just close your eyes
And feel the warmth of the sun
You can feel the light and the life
So only the ONE can touch you

Swim in the ocean or in the river
Feel how the water is softly playing around you
It is completely soaking you
And is completely enclosing you
But it never it will confine you
Only HE can be like that with you

Or stroke very softly
The coat of the bumblebee
So silky, so velvetlike
So immense is this miracle
All your doubts will cease
Just through this experience
And you know this can only HE show you

Feel how the wind is sweeping through the area
And touching leaves and grass
It is fluttering around you
And sometimes it is in harmony with you
Nevertheless the wind

Is tied to nothing and to nobody
It is so free and at the same time
So completely surrendering
You are able to feel it
But never will you be able to hold it
Only He can be like this with you

Would you like to know how God tastes?
Would you like to know how delicious HE is?
He is the finest, the best
Think about fruits, nuts and berries
And you no longer can ignore it
You will feel thankfulness for this

In which form is HE hiding himself?
Do you know it?
I think your curiosity will now rise
Would you like to know what God looks like?
Just look at the corn
So small, so solid and so powerful
Like this can only be the ONE

Or the stars so far
And at the same time so close to you
So close, that you can nearly touch them
So shiny, so gleaming and so pure
So only can be HE

The tree shows us what is harmony
It also shows the change of the seasons
It is steadfast, enduring and it gives freely
The tree is silent and wise
It is perfect and perfect can only be HE

The crystal in the hills
Is patiently growing towards the sun
It is waiting for nothing
And silently accepts its fate
So patient can only be HE

Close your eyes and see the Light within
So clear, so pure and so shiny in the darkness
So sparkling for you
Only HE is able to do this

You take care of the rose and put it in water and you admire it. You can hardly belief this beauty. Some days later you will see a new leaf is sprouting on the bush. Yet something better will happen! There are not only leaves that you can see. Short time later you will be completely astonished for now there will be sprouting some very lovely buds.

You know that game between you and the bush has gone on for some years now already. And still every time you cannot believe it. It is always a new miracle for you to see.

Science likes to explain and to prove everything. That's why they are doing such wild experiments, enthusiastically absorbed. They have no idea that you don't need to prove God. This knowledge is already in your heart.

You are smiling inwardly. Science is also coming from God, but it would be great if they made no longer experiments with animals and if their habits weren't sometimes so barbarous. It seems that many people have forgotten that God is within all creatures. So, I would wish that they wouldn't force rivers into new beds and would no longer interfere with nature so we would again be able to live like in paradise.

When, when will it be like this?

It would be so nice if everyone accepted nature and each other and no longer tried to make everything better.

Everything is already perfect, because it is made by God.

One of God's lovely and perfect Creatures.

Your Master

He carries you to the highest summits and suddenly He lets you fall down deeply. With this kind of test you suddenly get rid of every silly idea. You are hanging in the middle, you are not pure, you are not light, you are not bad, not impure, nothing of all this, but you are just not pure enough.

While falling down you are trying to process all sorts of thoughts. You think it should never happen again that you fall down so deep and you immediately start to practice during the fall and you remember again your Mantra, Pranayama and positive thinking and you practice like a frantic one. By the time you come to the next summit you will have forgotten everything again.

You think you are full of Bhakti for Him. But in fact you will not look so correctly within, because you are afraid to recognize that maybe you don't have enough Bhakti.

If you are filled with Bhakti for Him then you will burn off your feet, only to be close to Him. And you will not be permanently caught in your own thoughts. You will practice and learn and follow His advice. You will not protect your ego and take care of it so much. Then you will not always remain in the same place, and you will recognize what your master is expecting from you and what He will like to give to you.

Then He is our Light and we are His stars. He loves us all; He gladly loves us so much. But He doesn't like one thing. He does not like cloudy stars! That's why He is cleaning us, scrubbing us and dipping and polishing us. Sometimes you can also see Him angry if the dust stays within us. He works on us as long as we are not pure enough. He works on us until we are shiny, sparkling and flashing. In this work He is sweating and perspiring, because it is so difficult purifying us.

If you want to make His work easier, practice, practice and practice! Develop devotion and fill yourself completely with love. Then you will soon twinkle and sparkle. You will reflect His Light, Knowledge and His Love and finally you will be able to become one with HIM.

What is Karma?

There are many people with lots of difficulties in their lives. It seems that they have only sorrows and painful times. You watch when from a distance, when you are not involved in the situation, then you only think what difficult lives those people have, what difficult karma. If it is not our karma, if we are not in this difficult situation ourselves, then it is very easy to talk and forget about it very quickly.

But what when we look into our own lives? What is karma? Is it simply just a reaction to a former action? Where does karma begin and where does it end? What is it really? When the matter is rotating round about our life then we cannot see it. We can't see the reasons, because if we are in difficulties fear blocks us up. Perhaps everything about karma in my life will be clearer for me if I write my thoughts and my feelings from my life experience.

I am practising yoga and I have the feeling that yoga is awakening me. I have the feeling that just now I am starting to live. Just now I am conscious that for my whole life I have been searching for spirituality, searching for divine knowledge.

When did it begin? At what time was a longing for this knowledge awakened in me?

My childhood was a very good one. I grew up in the countryside, close to a river. At that time the water was completely clear and fresh. I remember very well. I am still feeling its marvellous freshness and its scent and will never forget it. I could feel the water and experienced it with all the animals and plants that belonged to it.

In my childhood we used to play at the riverside and also in the water. I was still very small, 4 - 5 years old, not yet in school. One day I was watching the fish and tried to catch them by standing in the water. All of a sudden I lost my balance; my feet couldn't reach the ground anymore. My small body was turned around and around, pulled under the water. I couldn't swim yet. I just couldn't get hold of the ground. I felt I was drowning. The time seemed endless, but I was not afraid at all. Then I gave up fighting for my life. As soon as I no longer fought for my life, all of a sudden I was standing on firm ground.

I went back to the river bank. My consciousness and my little world had changed. It was a change that made me very happy.

Was this karma? I don't mean my nearly drowning. No, but this has probably been one of the big changes in my life. I think of the kind of bliss which I felt. It was the first time that I had felt this happiness.

A few years later it happened again. I almost drowned again. Still I was not able to swim. Again we were at the river playing inside and outside the water. It was an especially beautiful summer day. In the shadow it was pleasant and breezy. We were watching the dragonflies dancing. I enjoyed it deeply. Naturally, I also went into the water. I was about 12 years old. Again I lost my balance and couldn't get my feet on the ground. And again I was fighting for my life. Nevertheless I stayed calm and peaceful. And again I managed to reach the bank of the river. Nobody had watched it. Sitting in the sun I observed myself. And again there was another big change within me. A new window had opened in me. There was sudden knowledge about divine reality in me. Was this karma?

Until now I never have spoken about this, not even with my mother. Nobody would understand this kind of feeling. We are judging other people too quickly. Why is somebody not doing something in this way, why is he or she doing it in that way? I try not to judge at all. I try to give up such habits. I try to take my fellow men as they are; I try to accept them as they are. Sometimes it is very difficult. But who can really feel what is going on inside other people? Nobody can. We try to feel what is working within others and we try to understand them, but we are not able to have the same feeling or pain. It is not possible. The big changes in our lives which really change us cannot be seen from the outside. This is because it happens within our souls, our hearts and our feelings. Only we know it and nobody else.

Is this karma what happens inside of people? What are we thinking and feeling, which we cannot see from outside?

Once I was standing in a traffic jam in the middle of a city. Suddenly I heard a sphere sound. Everywhere around me this sphere sound was calling my name. Again and again it called it. These were such joyful voices; it was so beautiful, so indescribable and wonderful. Even now I can still remember the magnificence of those sounds. Was this karma?

Did angels call my name? Did my Master call me? I think everyone would like to be called by their protecting angel or their master, with such high spirits and cheerful voices. But the way to the Master is a hard and difficult inner way. To give up ego is very painful. But if you are ready for it, if you are ready to be a devotee, if you are ready to understand, then your Master will find you.

This is exactly what happened to me at that time. To prepare ourselves we have to go the way of love and understanding for each other. Also we have to have in us the longing to reach God.

Otherwise there is no way to receive divine knowledge.

If we are only curious we will get a Master who is just satisfying our wishes. Not much more can happen, because a Master likes to make us happy but also to give us all his Divine Knowledge. But if we are not ready we are not able to take it.

The door to the Master is always wide open, we only have to step in and work on ourselves, and then we will receive any kind of help. Mostly it fails because we have too much fear to make changes in our lives. Is this fear coming from our karma?

My husband's life at the end had depended on a machine. Was it his karma, or was it mine? I believe in rebirth. Had he returned again to earth with this difficult fate to complete his learning process and mine too? If so, then there must have been great love between us from lives before.

All these thoughts very often are on my mind, but still I am sometimes not very thankful.

I met a person with healing energy. She was a healer from the Philippines. Actually my husband was receiving treatment from her. I only accompanied him, because I was very curious and wanted to be with him. After she had treated my husband I began to cry and I didn't know why. There was no reason, but I cried and cried and could not stop it. Inside I was very happy but still crying! I also had the feeling that I was a pot with boiling water and the steam was going out. The steam was my tears. Again I felt the kind of happiness I had felt when I nearly drowned. Was this karma that I met the woman with the healing energy?

This woman presented me with her prayer and this prayer was a request to God for protection so that we take the right path. Was it karma to get this prayer in that moment?

She was nearly three months in our city and I was able to meet her five or six times. Verbally we were not able to communicate, but our souls and hearts had the same aim and we felt that we were one.

When she was gone I suddenly longed to practice yoga. I was looking for a place and came to Swamiji. Was it karma?

I think in the first half year after my decision to take the spiritual path I fought with the inner difficulties I had had all may life. That kind of decision we have to take by ourselves, nobody can take it for us. No others are responsible for us; we are the ones who are responsible for ourselves. But the longing to take the spiritual path was so strong that I decided to do it seriously. For me it was very clear that it could happen only with a Master who guides my. Was this karma that I decided to take seriously the spiritual path?

While doing sports or taking walks through nature, I often wonder if mother earth can feel us human beings in the same way we feel a fly crawl over our skin. Is she able to perceive us, to observe us? Does that kind of thinking come from karma?

Once I was watching a butterfly flying against the window. It was already completely exhausted. I stretched out my finger towards it, closed my eyes and told him in my mind: "Sit on my finger and I will take you to the open air". After some seconds he sat down on my finger. I opened my eyes and held my finger out of the window. The butterfly flew away and I was so surprised and happy that a butterfly was able with so much power to balance on my finger. The butterfly had trusted me and wasn't afraid of me.

In the same way the butterfly trusted me we would need to trust the guidance of the Master. Is it karma to trust so strongly?

My thoughts about karma started when I did not know how to deal with grain moths. One day I found many in my cereal and didn't know to deal with them. What will happen to me, when I just kill them? My life experience was that I already knew that whatever I do will be returned to me. After, considering this for a while I decided to concentrate on this matter and sent to the grain moths my message that they were welcome. But please don't place eggs anywhere! They didn't like this kind of thinking and one day they just disappeared and never came back.

Generally I'm connecting the word karma with happiness. All right, I also suffer sometimes, but I know it is always my own mistake, because I should forgive everything that people do to me. Sometimes it just needs some time until I am able to do so.

As I write them down my thoughts about karma are very simple. What do I want to achieve by my writing? I would like to give some inspiration. I would like to encourage people to think in a new way about their own lives. I would like to encourage people to read and understand my thoughts with their heart and to think in a positive way about their own destinies.

Many people just stick to their way of thinking about themselves and they are much afraid to change it. But if we try to find new ways to think about ourselves, then we mostly are also able to see the good side of situations. Everything, every situation has a good teaching and a good side for us too.

It is good to learn to think in a positive way about everything and that is already Yoga, as the word Yoga means also to balance. If we are able to forgive ourselves then we are able to forgive our "pain-makers". When we are more peaceful within ourselves, we will radiate this to others and there will not be so much fighting within and around us.

I would like to inspire other people to try to accept their lives, to force everybody seriously to cope as well as possible with tricky moments, und not to give up trying to be good, to be aware and not to harm others. It is bad enough that it sometimes just happens that we are harming others in our ignorance, victimizing or injuring them. However if we are doing this knowingly it is definitely bad for us. It will make no difference whether we think or act in a bad way.

If we are doing bad things, it will finally affect only ourselves. This also concerns plants and animals.

Karma will not leave us after we have died. Only the body will go, but karma will always stay with our being. It stays with our souls. It is like a shadow following us. It will follow us to the next life, and again we will have to work on it and try to purify it. It is very important to be good and not to make new bad karma. I think to work off the bad parts of our fate takes enough energy from us and it is really important not to create a new bad karma.

Now I am again at the beginning. Which is my karma? What do I have to work at, and to purify?

Maybe I should also speak about the pain and fighting that was sometimes within me. I was not only happy; sometimes I was also very, very desperate, unhappy and sad. My tears were not only tears of happiness. I have made enough mistakes in my life. Nevertheless I think I am lucky. There was hunger within me for being better and better. For that I work determinedly with mind and body. This gives me a feeling of satisfaction: knowing that I am on the right path.

Where there is a lot of pain there is also much happiness and satisfaction, once the working process is over. The pain will be forgotten very quickly but the feeling of joy and happiness will last.

Because of that, someone who begins to take the spiritual path, to search for higher vibrations, divine knowledge and purity cannot turn away from this path any more.

No matter what happens in their lives, people will always come back and try again to get further. We become dependent on higher vibrations. We become dependent on the feeling of peace and harmony. This kind of addiction will take us to God.

There are many people who are dependent on alcohol or all sorts of drugs. They are dependent because they are searching for something. But they don't know what they are searching for, they are hungry for something and they are missing it. Therefore they are searching in vain.

What is it that humans are searching for? Humans are searching for their origin, they are searching for God

Dharma Samrata Paramhansa
Swami Madhavananda Puriji, known as Holy Guruji

My Master: Mahamandaleshwar Paramhansa
Swami Maheshwarananda Puri Ji, known as Swamiji

Glossary

Asana	*yoga posture*
Ashram	*monastery*
Anand	*bliss, happiness*
Bliss	*happiness*
Bhajan	*spiritual or devotional song*
Bhakti	*unconditional love*
Dhoti	*cloth winding around the hips and legs. It looks like trousers*
Guru	*master*
Gurukripa	*mercy, grace of the master*
Karma	*actions, deeds*
Kurta	*long shirt*
Mahasamadhi	*when a yogi dies*
Mantra	*holy syllables, hymns, words or sentences through which spiritual and mental powers and talents are developed*
Om	*the original sound of the universe symbolising past, present and future*
Param	*supreme*
Paramhansa	*supreme soul*
Prasad	*blessed food*
Satsang	*Sat = truth, sang = being together (being together with a spiritual developed person)*
Siddhi	*Extraordinary power of the soul. Awaken naturally through spiritual maturity and yogic sadhana (exercises).*
Shraddha	*confidence*